For a Chance to Walk on Streets of Gold

poems by

Claire Weiner

Finishing Line Press
Georgetown, Kentucky

For a Chance to Walk on Streets of Gold

ACKNOWLEDGMENTS

 I would like to thank the following editors for their publication of individual
poems in previous versions:

"Beets" published as "Changing my Mind about Beets 1951—Now": *After
Hours*
"For a Chance" published as "The More Things Change, The More They Stay
the Same": *Peninsula Poets*
"While my Mother Sits Sewing" published in *Voices of Lincoln 2022 Poetry
Contest Winners Chapbook*
"Ode to My Husband's Hearing Aids" appeared in *Hoffman Center
Community Writes*
"Amber Beads" appeared in *PoetTreeTown Ann Arbor*

Publisher: Leah Huete de Maines
Editor: Christen Kincaid
Cover Art: Stephen Haskin
Author Photo: Joni Strickfaden, Strickfaden Photography LLC
Cover Design: Elizabeth Maines McCleavy

Order online: www.finishinglinepress.com
also available on amazon.com

Author inquiries and mail orders:
Finishing Line Press
PO Box 1626
Georgetown, Kentucky 40324
USA

Contents

For my parents who made these poems possible
and for Kirk, Nathan, Anna
and Samuel

For a chance

To walk on streets
paved with gold,

refugees ride waves
of half-empty
promises,

sleep in dust
that belongs
to no country.

In Poland and Russia,
land was traded
like marbles

and the tzar's soldiers
galloped through shtetls
snatching Jews with delight.

My grandfathers sailed
to a new world with, I'm told,
"Nothing but the clothes on their backs."

One a tailor, one a blacksmith,
they boarded ships as Nuchem
and Hershel, found the way

to Chicago, shed names
as they went— disembarking
as Nathan and Harry,

never imagining
a future—war after war—
incinerated bodies

ash settling
in every nook
and cranny.

Kilbourne Avenue

—Lincolnwood, Illinois 1950s

I.   7348 Kilbourne Avenue

Margie's parents held hands
summer nights, listened for crickets,
toads, looked for constellations.

Her dad taught earth science
at a local college, so he knew
interesting stuff. Her mom

gazed up with him, listened
to his every word. Margie and I
skipped behind them,

giggling at their romance
pretending her mom and dad
were Barbie and Ken.

II.   7345 Kilbourne Avenue

Strains of Frank Sinatra
rippled across a grass path
between our brick houses.

I knew Fannie and Phil were
fox trotting to *The Best Was Yet To Come*.
Phil owned a poultry business.

He killed chickens all day,
but Fannie always swooned
when he walked in the door

smelling of blood and guts,
"Phil, you sweetheart, shower
before you kiss me."

III.   7343 Kilbourne Avenue

I never dreamt my parents
were Barbie and Ken
but I wished they were.

My mother tall, slim,
wearing a ball gown
or a black and white striped

bathing suit, no
thought to the 4-inch, black,
high-heeled pumps.

How they might hurt her back or hips.

My father even taller, slim,
no scars on his back or knee,
no brother to support,

no job to hate, no moods to swing
no wife to misunderstand, no arteries
to clog, or heart to fail.

Leaning in, touching hands
as though they were made
for just each other.

At the Top of the Stairs

At the top of the stairs,
I dared myself not to listen

to whispers from
my parents' bedroom.

Always at the end
of his workday.

Her voice coiled, taut—
his uncertain, hushed.

I would reach for the knots
of beige wool carpet—

suburban worry beads
between my fingers—

jumping up at the sound
of their bedroom door opening,

all of us pretending.

Not Once

Not once did anyone tell me
why my father sat in our Queen Anne
chair in the living room, mornings

before work—his head heavy,
as though cradled by
wings.

Or why he came home early,
went to the bedroom,
to rest.

I would listen through the door
to my father's whisper, my mother's
knotted voice.

Not once, did I see my mother wipe
a cold sweat of worry, or hear my father's
apologies, swimming with shame.

Not once did my father raise his voice
or hand to me or my mother. I saw my mother
give my father *How to Win Friends and Influence People.*

I saw my father put it under his stack
of dog-eared *Saturday Reviews,*
National Geographics.

I heard lamentations from my father's
violin rise from the wood paneled, basement-
turned-family room.

My father called me his kitten as I curled
next to him on the couch when we watched
Bonanza or *Wonderful World of Disney.*

Just once, he bought a box of Cuban
cigars for a thousand
bucks to give to friends. Contraband.

Just once, he bought a red,
Chevy Malibu convertible
on a Tuesday after work.

Just once he brought home
a full-length mink coat for my mother.
She stroked the fur, adoring it.

Not once did anyone
tell me this was illness.

While My Mother Sits Sewing

I wake feverish; her scent surrounds me.
She stitches oases from scarce pieces
her fingers fluid, in full swing,
each stitch second to none.

She stitches oases from scarce pieces.
Scissors shear scattered remnants,
each stitch second to none,
silver flashes of nimble needle.

Scissors shear scattered remnants.
The push pull of threads in and out—
silver flashes of nimble needle—
bits of ribbons wave like wishes.

Pull push of threads in and out
her brow crinkles like paper patterns.
Bits of ribbon wave like wishes,
my mother's forgone dreams.

Her brow crinkles like paper patterns.
Laboring hands ward off
my mother's forgone dreams.
I watch feverish; her scent surrounds me.

Beets

I can't stand to look at the bloodiness
of the beets—like decapitated, balding
gnomes, their botched features
trimmed with hairy roots.

But after I pull hard, but not too hard.
on the chrome handle of the white
Frigidaire, they're impossible to ignore.

They compete for space on the middle shelf
sandwiched, between the ordinary—a gallon
of whole milk, last night's roast chicken, green olives,
a jar of creamed herring. All controlled by my mother.

I fear their misshapen forms will soon appear
on the dinner table—a melamine platter
full of gaping wounds
the result of primordial battle.

> *"But why don't you like them?*
> *They're good for you.*
> *Just a sip of borscht, with a dollop of sour cream.*
> *I made it just for you."*

Daddy delights in the Russian-ness of them,
they remind him of his mother, of Maxwell Street,
and the Jewish diaspora in Chicago.
But sometimes he breaks Rabbinic rules and makes
me ham and cheese on Jewish rye.

> *"I don't care if I have to sit at the table until tomorrow.*
> *You can't make me eat those godforsaken, shrunken heads.*
> *Solid or liquid, I don't care, even if Daddy loves them."*

If your kidneys hadn't failed at ninety-two, Mom,
we'd have this conversation now, right now.
You would deny our history of beet battles,
your memory always sharp, not full of lies or delusion.

Now, at the Farmer's Market, I look sideways
at the gnarly mounds—red, yellow, white beets—
topped with generous, deep green leaves.

Each time I walk past a row,
I pass, move on to safe, unconflicted
vegetables. I fill my bags with calm lettuce,
harmless tomatoes, sturdy carrots.

Yet, I circle back, tempted,
lured by the whisper.

I hear rooted plants calling to me.

Holy Sundays

Like an ancient messenger,
he left early
most Sunday mornings.

With dawn his only
companion, he traveled,
not to the closest shops

but to the three where he deemed
the art of mixing, kneading, boiling,
and baking bagels was unsurpassed.

They knew him at Levinsons,
Ashkenazi's, and Manny's—
where the sign over the front
door invited customers to
kosher yiddish essen.

He chose several dozen holy delicacies—
plain, onion, sesame, poppy,
rye, and pumpernickel

and began his anonymous deliveries.
Neither hail, nor sleet, nor heat
in the Windy City stopped him.

No knock.
No note.
No doorbell.
Just a bag of bagels.

Left at the doors of friends
and neighbors who finally
figured out their Sunday morning
hero was none other

than my father.

Her Memory Be a Blessing
For Molly Factor

Dear Bubbe,

I spent the day searching
for you, clicking on my laptop,

so desperate to find a trace
my fingers almost bled.

All I have is a single black & white photo—
you seated, an armchair, whisps of hair escaping

from your bun. The faded date, *1953,*
means you were already my grandmother.
And now I'm a grandmother, too.

I was only five when you died,
but I remember:
fried onions and potatoes
your generous lap, your fleshiness,
hard candies we kept secret.
We communicated with hugs
because you only spoke Yiddish.

There's so much I'll never know. Daddy didn't talk much
about his family other than, "It was hard for them."

Only once he drove to Maxwell Street to show me where
he'd lived as a boy—where Zaide worked as a blacksmith,
where the kosher butcher and shul were.

You didn't smile often. But why would you?
Had you heard hoofbeats of the Tzar's soldiers?
Had they rumbled through your village, your house?
Had you felt their calloused hands on your skin?

Or had bad news simply traveled fast before you landed
at Ellis Island in 1909, like so many other hopefuls,
where you surrendered your roots and even your name—

Malke Factorowicz Weinerman
to become
Molly Factor Weiner.

When I Was Sure of His Love

And when I was sure enough
of his heart's goodness, I told
him the story of my father,
the gentlest of souls.

I told him of jokes mailed
to comedians—Jack Benny, Jerry Lewis,
Milton Berle and the rest—and autographed thank-yous
in return.

I told him of contraband Cuban cigars,
Saturday afternoons at the opera in our basement-
turned-rec room,

playing poker for frilled toothpicks
at the kitchen table, backrubs when I was sick,
and of blueberry pancakes on Sunday

mornings—just us two early risers—
of forbidden ham and cheese on Jewish rye
and the Odyssean search for perfect cole slaw.

I told of my father who sat too often
in the living room chair—
praying for ambition that was always just out of reach,
how my mother didn't understand.

And of the long, crooked scar on my father's back,
the small one on his knee, the life-saving ones
on his thigh and chest where they switched out
bad artery for good suddenly one Monday morning.

I told him of the endless night that descended
on my father after he was brought back
from the dead that Monday, how my sister and I
visited him in a psych ward. My mother too ashamed to go.

I told him of my father's apology, so hushed we
could barely hear, his eyes overflowing
with shame. In the elevator, my sister
and I hugged and sobbed. I was twenty-one.

When I finished unraveling
the tale of my father, he looked
at me with the gentleness
of dawn.

Then, I was sure.
And we lay together.

Ode to my husband's hearing aids

Sorcerer of sound, Eros
whose arrow points directly
into my beloved's ears,
I adore you.

Minuscule, featherweight, miracle!
You rest so lightly on the flesh of ear canals,
transmit sound in a way utterly beyond me.

You perform your magic so quietly.
No cheering crowds, no minions in the
in the wings. In fact, you do your
meticulous work while camouflaged.

You gather my words
instantaneously, convert them
into mysterious codes.
You amplify them, loud as a giant.
Then, you sweep your magic wand,
codes become waves, rush into his ears
pulse through curlicue canals, bang
into a drum, dance through an elaborate
labyrinth of hammer, anvil, stirrup,
end in a snail touched by a special nerve.

Our forty-year conversation continues
at the well-worn oak dining table in Michigan
or under a sprawling Palo Verde in Tucson,
without a "huh" or "what."

If not for you, our long love affair might have
shattered, not for change of heart, but for
change of hearing. All my sweet nothings turned
to sweet nothing.

My Kitchen Table

Your sturdiness, your dark oaken stability, was all I needed.
How can I thank you enough for all you've done?

When we met in L.A. in that dusty antique store,
we were both far from home.

You were from a smoke-filled pub in the U.K.,
where the world was being pieced together after the Blitz.
I was from a post-war, split-level in the Midwest
where children's fingerprints were wiped off walls.

But once I spied you and claimed you, we've never strayed.

Just last night you offered us homegrown tomatoes,
sweet corn, grilled salmon— a late summer's blessing.
Cups of Earl Grey this morning as we searched
for hidden crossword answers, just for fun.

And now, patience while I wrestle with these very words.

The chairs we bought to accompany you are long gone.
But you didn't bat an eyelid when we introduced the new
foursome.

Do you remember the one dreadful December
night when my husband and I were perched
on the edge of middle-age indifference to each other?

You kept us from falling.

And for gathering our family during the storms of door
slamming,
eye-rolling adolescence—even if your only offering was
frozen pizza.

It was always enough.

My Mother's Fall

I wonder about the moment
before my mother fell

while brushing her teeth
in a blue tiled bathroom
in a Florida retirement home.

The doctor said her femur
crumbled—honeycombed
with fragility, brittleness
hidden just under the skin.

I wonder had she slept soundly
the night before. Or not at all?

Did she feel the usual knot of worry
about money somewhere in her gut?

Did she hear my father's sweet
tenor voice echoing in her memory?

Maybe she was simply planning
the day—solving a puzzle,
a bridge game, lunch with friends

when her bone shattered
to be held together
with rods and pins

but never to be the same.

Penultimate hospital visit

Pastel nothing, shifting colors
of fluorescence, the engineered drip, drip, drip.

I'd spent years going in and out of rooms like these.
I wasn't put off.

My mother was propped on pillows
like the Victorian heroine she never was. Her left hand—
cool,
desiccated, translucent.

She squeezed my fingers, whispered, "You're here."

A nurse zipped in, busying herself adjusting this,
measuring that. "You must be the daughter," she said.

I looked at my mother—white as milk,
answers to the Times crossword

behind her closed eyes and remembered
the way people used to say we looked alike.

Talking to the dead

My oldest friend talks
to her dead parents. Calls
them by their first names—
Bobbie and Sam.

Her house overflows
with their Coltrane & Mingus,
tablecloths, wooden
salad bowl, silver candlesticks.

She hears their laughs, feels
warmth around their oak table.
Sees Sam guide Bobbie
across the dance floor,

his hand gentle on her back,
her head at home on his
shoulder, how he never missed
a chance to sweep her off her feet.

Her home is papered with photographs
of them—windowsills, dresser
tops, refrigerator magnets—
in the blush of first love, wizened with age.

She never misses a chance
to light a candle or sanctify
their memory.

But I don't remember my parents
in silver-filigreed frames,
with stuff on shelves, faded letters
of devotion bound with ribbons in a drawer.

Long ago I stopped collecting
memories, saying blessings.

Yet, when *I lie down and when I rise up,*

I see my mother's wrist— gold
charms jangling, my father's hands

gliding the bow of his violin
towards the slow echo of Barber's *Adagio for Strings.*

Amber Beads

They have waited
generations, traveled
oceans to you,

these beads handed
to me by my mother,
handed to her by hers.

Let them drip
between your fingers,
feel the heat of their history,

the flow of ancestors
coursing through
your veins.

They are not only gems
to rest upon your sternum,
dangle from your ears,

or encircle your wrist.
They are your legacy,
your lantern.

Can you see how the splintered
Baltic suns illuminate
your unknown path?

With Thanks

I am grateful to so many who believed I had something to say and that I should say it.

Thank you to every writing group I have been fortunate to be a part of; some of them have been short-lived, but have been valuable, nonetheless. A special thank you to my Hugo House Alumni Group—you know who you are.

Thank you to University of Michigan Bear River Writers' Conference where I have found so many good friends and writers. Special thank you to Cody Walker, Tom Lynch and Richard Tillinghast.

Thank you to Zilka Joseph, poet mentor extraordinaire, Simone Yehuda, and Andrea Hansell. All of whom have supported my writing in important ways. And to my remarkable friends who have cheered me on along the way.

And of course, thank you to my dear husband Kirk, and our children Nathan and Anna who continue to amaze me each day.

Claire Weiner was born in Chicago and raised in the Chicago suburbs. She attended the University of Illinois Urbana-Champaign where she graduated Phi Beta Kappa, and then received a master's in social work from the University of Chicago. Except for a decade in Los Angeles, she has spent most of her adult life in Ann Arbor, Michigan. She spent her decades-long, non-writing career working as a psychotherapist, helping people make more sense of their life stories. She began writing in earnest when her children were grown. Her work has been published in *After Hours Press, Burningwood Literary Review, Uppagus, Muddy River Poetry Review, Pennisula Poets, Bear River Review* and others. She and her husband now split their time between Michigan and Arizona, grateful to be surrounded by natural beauty in both places.